Day of the Dead

A Latino Celebration of Family and Life

Carol Gnojewski

Enslow Elementary

an imprint of

Enslow Publishers, Inc.

40 Industrial Road	PO Box 38
Box 398	Aldershot
Berkeley Heights, NJ 07922	Hants GU12 6BP
USA	UK

http://www.enslow.com

To Olga Sanchez for her insights and her inspiring ability to make cultural events happen; and to my son Conrad for his writing assistance. Also, to the memory of my loved ones: Leona and William O'Neill and Aunt Faith.

Enslow Elementary, an imprint of Enslow Publishers, Inc.

Enslow Elementary® is a registered trademark of Enslow Publishers, Inc.

Copyright © 2005 by Carol Gnojewski

Library of Congress Cataloging-in-Publication Data

Gnojewski, Carol.
   Day of the Dead : a Latino celebration of family and life / Carol Gnojewski.
     p. cm. — (Finding out about holidays)
   Includes bibliographical references and index.
   ISBN 0-7660-1780-X
   1. All Souls' Day—Juvenile literature. 2. Mexico—Social life and customs—Juvenile literature. I. Title. II. Series.
   GT4995.A4G56 2004
   394.264—dc22

2004008714

Printed in the United States of America

10 9 8 7 6 5 4 3 2

To Our Readers: We have done our best to make sure that all Internet Addresses in this book were active and appropriate when we went to press. However, the author and publisher have no control over and assume no liability for the material available on those Internet sites or on other Web sites they may link to. Any comments or suggestions can be sent by e-mail to comments@enslow.com or to the address on the back cover.

Photo Credits: © 1996–2003 ArtToday, Inc., p. 1; © 1999 Artville, LLC., p. 12; Associated Press, pp. 5, 9, 10, 23, 24, 27, 29, 33, 34, 35, 41; Corel Corporation, pp. 13, 14, 15, 18, 20, 21, 32 (bottom), 37, 42–43 (background), 44, 48; Courtesy of Anne Enslow, pp. 4, 7, 16, 17, 22, 26, 30, 36, 38, 39, 40; Hemera Technologies, Inc. 1997–2000, pp. 2, 6, 25, 45; © 1996–2004 JupiterImages, pp. 3, 8, 11, 28, 31, 32 (top), 46, 47; Library of Congress, p. 19; Cathy Tardosky, pp. 42, 43.

Cover Photo: background, AP (Children in Chicago, Ill., carry traditional paper maiche skulls for a parade to celebrate Day of the Dead.); inset #1, © 1996-2004 JupiterImages; inset #2, Courtesy of Anne Enslow.

CONTENTS

Family members use flowers as decorations for the Day of the Dead celebrations.

CHAPTER 1

Day of the Dead

It is the afternoon on the first of November. In villages throughout Mexico, people prepare for a big picnic. Everyone is in a festive mood. Church bells toll. Fireworks pop and bang. They announce the arrival of special guests. The spirits of the dead are coming! Families carry *canastas*, or baskets, filled with food and cleaning supplies to the cemetery. They scrub and weed around the headstones of relatives. Once the graves are tidied, families sit

Mariachis sometimes walk along the graves singing to the dead.

together and eat. It is crowded in the cemetery. The whole town is there. Kids play games with friends. Musicians called *mariachis* stroll among the graves. They sing popular songs. People sell balloons and flowers outside the cemetery.

As night falls, candles are placed on the graves. There is one candle for each dead family member. One by one the candles are lighted. The names of the dead are said aloud. Shadows cast by the flickering candles dance from face to face and tomb to tomb. All night long, the picnic continues. Families stay awake and keep dead relatives company. They gossip and share family stories. They remember the good times they had with those who had died.

A family decorated this grave and will spend the night here to remember their dead relatives.

A boy scout places a flag at a headstone in a cemetery in Kentucky on Memorial Day. This is one way people in the United States remember their loved ones.

In the United States, death is not always openly talked about. When a person dies, there are services held before the burial. Cemeteries are sometimes located far away from city centers. After dark, they are not meeting places for the living. To people in the United States, spending the night in a

The Days of the Dead are a time to remember those who have died. This family is decorating the grave of a loved one with a layer of flower petals.

People in Mexico celebrate the Days of the Dead over several nights and days.

cemetery may sound like a scene in a scary Halloween movie. It is not thought of as scary in Mexico. Picnicking with dead relatives is one way that many Mexicans celebrate a sacred holiday called *Los Días de los Muertos*. In the Spanish language this stands for the Days of the Dead. Sometimes Days of the Dead is called Day of the Dead.

The Days of the Dead are celebrated from October 31 to November 2. This is an important holiday in Mexico because it centers on the family and on the stages of life and death. Since ancient times, Mexicans have set aside these days for spiritual and family healing.

Skeletons and skulls are symbols of the Day of the Dead.

The Aztecs built a great empire in what is now Mexico.

CHAPTER 2

Ancient Aztec Beliefs

The Aztecs were among ancient people who built great empires in what is now the country of Mexico. The Aztecs saw that the growing season came and went in a regular cycle. Stars also changed positions in a set way that they could remember and record. Their interest in the sky led the Aztecs to make a solar calendar. The Aztec calendar is sometimes called the Sun Calendar. It is a large disk made of green volcanic stone. The disk shows time in a series of circles with the sun in the center. There are

The Aztecs made statues of what they thought the gods looked like. This is the Rain God.

circles within circles. This meant that time and life repeated itself.

Tonatiuh, the sun, was one of many *teotl*, or gods, that the Aztecs worshipped. They believed it was the giver of life. Tonatiuh died each evening to make night possible. So, to the Aztecs, that meant people died to make room for others. Aztecs understood human life as a cycle that did not end in death. Though a person's body was buried in the ground, his or her spirit lived on. Souls entered worlds hidden from the living. It mattered how someone died, and not how he or she lived. Dead warriors became hummingbirds and flew to the sun. Babies went to a land where milk dripped from trees. There was even a special place for people who drowned or were struck by lightning.

Most souls walked along an endless road called *Mictlán*. This was the underworld. Clothing, tools, and cooking pots were buried with them for use on their journey. The Lord of Death, *Mictlantecuhtli*, guarded their bones. The Aztecs feared him. However, they did not think him evil. He was both greedy and generous. He had the power to create life or to take it away.

The Aztecs thought that when night ends, the sun is reborn. The Aztecs believed that the dead would rise again, too. They believed that dead bodies waited for rebirth like seeds in the soil. Festivals for the dead were held throughout the year in the ninth and tenth months of

This ancient ruin was a temple built for the Sun God and is called the Pyramid of the Sun.

Masks are still worn today for the Day of the Dead as seen on this little girl in Oaxaca, Mexico.

the Sun Calendar. These months fell in late summer. Wealthy families shared food with poorer families. They also invited the dead spirits to visit them.

Since these souls had passed on to a new level of the universe, the Aztecs treated them like gods. Strong incense called *copal* was burned. Copal is made from tree sap. The Aztecs imagined its smoke reached Mictlán. It led the dead from Mictlán to the homes of family and friends. Shrines for the dead were decorated with bark paper called *amatl*. Newly harvested fruits, vegetables, and flowers were heaped upon them.

Altars like this one were made to honor the dead.

The Spanish conquered and destroyed most of the Aztec buildings to make room for their own. These Aztec ruins can be found in Mexico City, Mexico.

CHAPTER 3

Spanish Conquest

In 1521, Spanish soldiers conquered Mexico. They overthrew the Aztec Empire and took over the Aztec cities. Mexico became a Spanish colony. Many Aztecs were enslaved. The soldiers wanted to get rid of the Aztec way of life. First, they tore down the Aztec temples and built Spanish churches on the same ground. Then they brought in Spanish priests called missionaries. Missionaries taught the Aztecs about the Catholic religion. They hoped it would replace their ancient beliefs. The Catholic Church was very powerful at this time.

The Spanish tried
to make the Aztecs
believe in Christianity.

The Spanish missionaries worshipped one God instead of many. They believed in an afterlife for the soul. Souls were judged at death for their deeds in life.

The missionaries tried to teach Christianity to the Aztecs. They taught them about the lives of Catholic saints and martyrs. Some people with a special relationship to God became saints. Martyrs had been killed for their Christian beliefs. The missionaries compared saints and martyrs to the Aztec gods of the upper and lower worlds.

Like the Aztecs, Spanish missionaries honored the dead on special days such as

All Saints' Day, which is November 1. Showing respect to the saints on this day was thought to bring protection to the living. November 2 is All Souls' Day. This festival began in Europe in the ninth century. On this day, the people of Spain asked God to send the souls of their loved ones to Heaven.

The Spanish missionaries would remember their loved ones in ceremonies.

Hernán Cortés and other Spanish soldiers attacked the Aztecs. The Spanish conquered the Aztec people and took their land.

They placed food and candles on family graves in churches and cemeteries. This custom closely matched the Aztec offering.

Mexico became independent from Spain in 1821. For three hundred years, Aztecs and other Mexican people tried to keep their beliefs separate from the Spanish. Yet over time, Spanish and Aztec traditions blended together. Now each region of Mexico has different ways of celebrating the Days of the Dead. One common practice is the making of an *ofrenda*, or altar. Ofrendas give families the chance to offer their love and to remember those who have died.

This woman places food as an offering on an altar.

Altars are set up in people's homes or in churches.

CHAPTER 4

My House Is Your House

Altars are special areas set up in people's homes. They can be tables, in a corner of a room, or anywhere space is available. In Aztec temples and in Spanish churches, gifts placed on the altars were meant for the gods. Altars can be found in many Spanish and Mexican homes. Families spend quiet moments around them singing and praying. Some fill an entire room. Others take up a corner of one. Home altars honor saints and family members. Photos, candles, religious statues, and prayer beads are often placed upon them.

DAY OF THE DEAD OFFERINGS

★

- *Papel picado—cut paper mat*
- *Candles—one for each dead family member*
- *Skulls made of wood or sugar*
- *Soap and small towel for washing*
- *Water jug with water for drinking*
- *Salt (symbol of life)*
- *Incense*
- *Bread*
- *Spicy foods*
- *Flowers*
- *Chocolate*

Not all altars are made the same. This one is made out of sand.

Everyone in the family gets involved in making an ofrenda for the Days of the Dead. First, they share memories about their dead relatives. What did they enjoy when they were alive? How did they dress? Which were their favorite movies, books, or snack foods? Next, things they liked or that belonged to them are placed on the altar. For example, if a dead relative was a guitar player, a real or a toy guitar might be added. Or the altar could be arranged in the shape of a guitar.

The ofrenda creates a space for the dead in a family's daily life. Dead relatives seem closer when their stories are retold. By making an ofrenda, families show each other how much dead loved ones still mean to them. Children learn their family history. They come to know all that their family has achieved together. Some families believe that the spirits themselves actually visit their homes during this time. In the state of Morelos, in Mexico, the altar is set up in a bedroom with chairs or a bed for the dead to rest on. The living then sleep on the front porch. This is not done out of fear. They want to make the dead comfortable.

Ofrendas may be set up outside the home. Some are placed near graves or on the very spot where a person died. In central Mexico, people build them on boats and barges. They float them down the canals. Museums and art galleries

Many families give up their beds for the night so their dead relatives will be more comfortable.

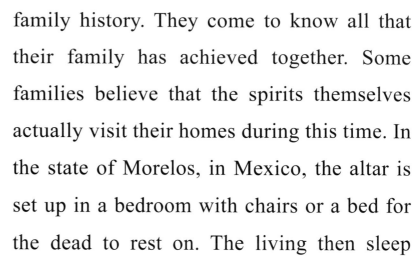

often honor famous people with large, fancy ofrendas. Churches and community centers may make simple ofrendas for people who are often forgotten, such as orphans and prisoners. In the *zócalos*,

or town squares of big cities, artists and activists create public altars that can be seen by everyone. These may point out conditions that need to be changed. Altars have been made for people who died of hunger, disease, or in unsafe workplaces.

Families ask musicians to play their dead loved one's favorite songs.

Marigolds are used to decorate altars.

CHAPTER 5

Fiesta, Flowers, and Food

Like the Aztec altars for the dead, modern ofrendas are heaped with symbols of the harvest. Most offerings include flowers. Marigolds, or *cempasuchitl*, are known as the flower of the dead. They are yellow-orange, and smell sharp and earthy. Their bright color and strong smell reminded the Aztecs of the sun. During the Days of the Dead, marigold flowers are arranged in vases, planted near graves, and strung onto cane wreaths or arches. The arches form a door for the dead to enter.

Food such as chili peppers and oranges are used as offerings at the altars.

Flower petals also are scattered over graves. Families make a path of seeds and petals from the cemetery to their homes. They expect the dead to follow this path. It is believed that marigolds are bright enough for the dead to see them after living in so much darkness.

Food is present on most altars, too. Market stalls are loaded with fresh fruits and vegetables. Families fill their baskets with oranges, chili peppers, tomatoes, and sugarcane. Some of these traditional foods are added directly to the altar. Others are made into rich and spicy dishes. Fruits, including pumpkin, are spiced or candied. Cornmeal is kneaded into dough and filled with meat or raisins to make tamales. Boiled cornmeal is sweetened with fruit juice for *atole*, a hot corn drink. *Mole* is a thick, slow-cooked sauce.

It is served with stewed turkey or chicken meat. In mole, cocoa beans are hand ground into cocoa powder and added to the sauce. The Aztecs were the first to use chocolate in their cooking.

No offering is complete without *pan de muertos*, or bread of the dead. This sweet egg bread is flavored with cinnamon or anise seed,

Bread is shaped into skeletons with candy faces.

This girl is stirring food that is being used as an offering. The photo on the altar shows people who are important to Mexican history. Pancho Villa (left center) and Emiliano Zapata (right center) led the Mexican Revolution in the early 1900s.

which tastes like black licorice. The bread is then glazed with honey or sprinkled with red or pink sugar. Sometimes the loaves are shaped like people or animals. This may mimic the Aztec custom of placing corn dough figures on temple altars. Skull-shaped pan de muertos is

another popular type of loaf. In some bakeries, dough is made into bones and baked atop round loaves.

Offerings of food make dead guests feel welcome in the homes of the living. The dead cannot really eat the food. They are thought to inhale its wonderful smell. When the dead leave, families make a meal of what is left on the altar.

Any act of eating is a form of sacrifice. All food comes from the dead bodies of plants and animals. In some places, people go from house to house and exchange food. As they hand it out they say to each other, "This is a gift from my dead relative." Legends warn that if you are not generous with your offering then bad luck will come to you in the coming year.

This girl places food on the graves of her brothers.

Skeletons have been a symbol of the Day of the Dead since the Aztecs.

CHAPTER 6

Skull Symbols

Stacked on candy store shelves, rows of sugar skulls look like tzompantli. These were racks that Aztecs used to dry out human skulls. Holes were drilled through the skulls so that they could be strung side by side on wooden rods like beads.

Skulls and skeletons are just as common as ofrendas during the Days of the Dead. Stores carry skeleton puppets, cutouts, and figurines. Skeleton toys wear clothes and are posed on everything from bicycles to barber chairs. These toys are based on the engravings of an artist named José Guadalupe Posada. Posada lived and worked in Mexico during the late 1800s. His art was printed in newspapers and pamphlets. Posada's skeletons are funny and not spooky. They remind us that skeletons support our bodies. Underneath our clothes and skin, we are all skeletons, too.

Children enjoy candy skulls as treats during the Day of the Dead.

Bakeries paint skeletons on their shop windows to advertise their holiday breads and cakes. They also sell skull-shaped treats made of chocolate or sugar. Sugar skulls are given as gifts. Families place them on the graves of young children. These unusual candies are covered with swirling icing patterns and shiny foil strips. Slips of paper with names written on them are attached to the candy forehead. You can eat a skull with your name on it or munch on one with the name of a friend.

In some neighborhoods, children go skulling. They travel from house to house carrying real or plastic pumpkins. At each door, they stop to recite funny verses called *calaveras*. The poems poke

Some children go skulling. They wear costumes and go door to door for treats.

Day of the Dead celebrations are passed down from parents to their children.

fun of famous people such as actors, athletes, and government leaders. Adults then hand out coins, nuts, or candy. This custom is called *calavereando*.

Two girls in New Mexico wear traditional puppets during a Day of the Dead Parade.

Hispanic communities throughout the United States celebrate the Days of the Dead. Their *fiestas*, or parties, may have candle-lighting ceremonies, altar making classes, and sugar skull decorating. For many Mexican Americans, this is a way of passing on their traditions to family and friends. It helps others take pride in their identity as they repeat, explore, and add to the ancient Mexican rituals handed down to them.

Day of the Dead Craft Project

★

Bendable Skeleton

You will need:

✔ **white pipe cleaners**

✔ **foam packing peanuts**

✔ **permanent black marker**

✔ **string (optional)**

*Safety Note: Be sure to ask for help from an adult, if needed, to complete this project.

1. Join two pipe cleaners at the center by twisting them together three times. This will make an X shape. The lower half of the X will form the legs of the skeleton and the upper half will be the body.

2. Form a small loop at the bottom of each leg and twist to make feet.

3. Twist the top halves together so they make one strand.

4. Bend the top half and twist together so that the body is thicker than the legs.

5. Form one small loop on each end of a third pipe cleaner. These are the skeleton's hands.

6. Place the third pipe cleaner perpendicular to the center of the body and twist to attach.

7. Draw a skeletal face onto a packing peanut using a permanent black marker.

8. Attach the head by inserting it onto the top of the body. Use a gentle, twisting motion or the peanut may break.

9. Bend the arms and legs into interesting poses.

If you wish, tie a length of string under the packing peanut skull and hang your skeleton near a Day of the Dead display. Or use the hand loops for hanging.

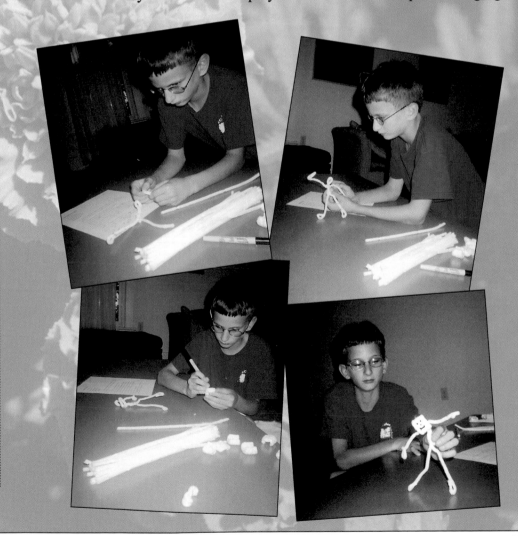

altar—A platform or table used as a center of worship.

Christianity— A religion based on the teachings of Jesus Christ.

missionary—A person sent to spread a religious faith.

tradition—The handing down of information or customs from parents to their children.

underworld—The place of departed souls.

Reading About

★

Ancona, George. *Pablo Remembers: The Fiesta of the Day of the Dead.* New York: Lothrop, Lee & Shepard Books, 1993. (Available in English and Spanish.)

DeAngelis, Gina. *Mexico.* Mankato, Minn.: Blue Earth Books, 2003.

Frost, Helen. *A Look at Mexico.* Mankato, Minn.: Pebble Books, 2002.

Hamilton, Janice. *Mexico in Pictures.* Minneapolis, Minn.: Lerner Publications Company, 2003.

Lowery, Linda. *Day of the Dead.* Minneapolis, Minn.: Carolrhoda Books, 2004.

San Vincente, Luis. *The Festival of Bones.* El Paso, Tex.: Cinco Puntos Press, 2002.

Wade, Mary D. *El Dia de los Muertos.* New York: Children's Press, 2002.

Internet Addresses

DAY OF THE DEAD

Learn more about Day of the Dead.
<http://www.elbalero.gob.mx/kids/about/html/
    holidays/ddead_kids.html>

MEXICO

*Click on the pictures to find out more about
    Mexico from this* Zoom School *Web site.*
<http://www.enchantedlearning.com/school/
    mexico>

Index

★

Index

★